Grit & Whimsy

Also by Karen Braucher Tobin

Heaven's Net
Sending Message Over Inconceivable Distances
Mermaid Café
Aqua Curves
Poetic License To Kill

Grit & Whimsy

Karen Braucher Tobin

© 2015 by Karen Braucher Tobin

All rights reserved. No part of this publication may be reproduced, stored in a retrieval system, distributed, or transmitted in any form, or by any means, including photocopying, recording, or other electronic or mechanical methods now available or that may become available in the future without the prior written permission of the publisher.

For permission requests, email the publisher at:
inquiry@cawingcrowpress.com

Published by:
Cawing Crow Press LLC
Dunlo, PA

ISBN: 978-1-68264-007-4

Library of Congress Control Number: 2015957630

Visit us on the web at: www.cawingcrowpress.com

Twenty of these poems performed by the author are available as an Audiobook, *Grit & Whimsy: Selected Poems*, produced by Cawing Crow Press, 2015. Sound design by Kyle Devine of Flatline Productions LLC, Portland, Oregon. Many thanks to Craig Grossman for his editorial expertise and guidance which improved these poems and to Kyle Devine for enhancing the spoken words with music and sound.

Contents

Why I Can't Go Back To My High-Tech Cubicle 1
Lifting Off 2
Yellow Orchids 3
A Spine Moving 4
Menopause 5
Autumn in the New Century 6
The Live-In 7
Queen Gluttony to Her Confessor 8
My Favorite Incarnations 9
Smitten with a Different Television 10
To Visit with the Grape Hyacinth 11
Tree Music 12
Spell of Enchantment 13
Brazen Hussy 14
Stone Heart 15
Never 16
My First Job 17
Russian Roulette 18
Inheritance 19
Before Our Minister's Child Rape Trial 20
Amethyst 22
Taking a Spin with Voltaire 23
The Swan Boats 25
OMG, Emily's on Facebook! 26
Sylvia Plath at 75 27
Stiff Gin & Tonics 28
The Prize 30
Iphigenia, Coming On Fast 31
Paleolithic Crone: The Beginning of Craft 32

Blue Kayak 33
Poem Written in a Copy of *The Aeneid* 35
When We Were Flying Fish 36
Couple with Ginger Lilies 37
Half a Valentine for Mister Wonderful 38
Dominatrix Month-by-Month Planner 39
The Tyranny of Women 40
Trumpet Flower Vine in August 41
Ars Poetica: A Charm of Hummingbirds 42
Hiking in the Sonoran Desert 44
Mona Lisa Discusses Money 45
Impossibly Huge Female 46
Because of Ouspensky 47
Kept 48
Locked-Up Girls 49
Astro-Girl! or, I've Been Reading Manga 50
Thirteen Noir Tweets 51
The View from Mt. Parnassus 52
Animation Moms 53
Scarecrow 54
Wasps 55
Panhandler Girl 56
Innocence Is Over Rated 58
Everything but a Paycheck 59
Blackbird's Wing 61
Our Anniversary 62
Fragment of Alaska 63
Higher Education 65
Without A Camera (Ghazal) 66
Yet Another Surprise 67

Buddha Out My Kitchen Window 68
Torso with Leaves 69
The Shape of River in His Hands 70
That Kitchen Bravery Thing 72
Acknowledgments 73
About the Author 75

"Many people have to change a lot, Govinda. They have to wear many robes. I am one of these, my friend. I welcome you, Govinda, and invite you to spend the night in my hut."

--Siddhartha, by Herman Hesse

Why I Can't Go Back To My High-Tech Cubicle

Vermilion, copper, lemon, jade — the Painter's colors penetrate
    my body.

Making love in Her sylvan boudoir, eating little, those are my
    cell phone and portfolios.

Lit incense sticks at shrines for the disappearing animals,
    those are my ruby and topaz diodes.

I'm done with make-up and high heels, left all my pinstripes behind.
    Autumn teaches me to travel light, a barefoot pilgrim.

Approve me or curse me: I praise Our Neuron Forest 24/7!

I streak down the radical path ecstatic humans have taken
    for millennia.

I don't steal. I hurt no one. Baby, why are you so threatened?

I've bodysurfed gargantuan waves and you want me to sit
    in a wading pool? For once, try to be deep.

Lifting Off

Sucked into a box, the mind is a dying river.
Fields of gray cubicles don't wake up.
Multifunctional MBAs like me zip by,
whisking cell phones, portable PCs.
I career down the conveyor belt,
eat food on plastic trays like the others.

How did I come
to this flat landscape —
thrumming, fluorescent,
all rectangles and no curves?
I try to move with the others.
I'm a twisted thing,
afraid of death yet dead.

There is a broken-winged force with a beak.
Part-woman, part-man, and predatory.
Will an animal fire enter me
so this broken-winged
shadow cannot scare me?
I hate calendars, clocks,
glib masks over lonely faces,
tubes, and metal enclosures.

I will become a hundred shades of green —
leaves, pine needles, lichen and moss.
Then the birds, showing black crests
and blue wings, will lift off
into their arc of revelry.

Yellow Orchids

> "Nobody sees a flower – really – it is so small it takes time - we haven't time…" -- Georgia O'Keefe

Nine flowers
      on a horizontal
           apple-green stem,

each canary flower
      a saffron girl in lemon dress
           with cinnamon bodice,

and a three-pronged
      tiger-stripe headdress
           of gold and ochre,

they came from jade curves —
      swerved thick cucumber green,
           digressed from pickle pods

out of cumin roots,
      straggling dank nutmeg
           zigzags below —

to dance honey & cream,
      apricot- & peach-skewered skirts
           held high.

A Spine Moving

In this poem there will not be
    a looming, joking male
        chiropractor
    who leans down and strikes
my twisted back
    as I scream. He will not tell me
        crazy stories about getting
    Cuban cigars for JFK as a young marine
as he checks
    the length of my legs. Afterward,
I will not float out of
        his office, completely without
    pain for two hours, seventeen minutes, thirty seconds.
There will not be hours. No three o'clock in the morning.
    No knocking the Ibuprofen
        to the floor in the dark bathroom.
    No muscle spasms that make me
        shriek. No hypodermics.
    No Tylenol. No physical therapy.
In this poem, a tall blond Finnish expert,
    my new Viking woman chiropractor,
        will not show me how
            one hip is higher than the other.
    No hip bones will be thumped. No necks
        whipped and cracked.
    No suggestion of future X-rays.
    No sitting down, lying down, or standing up;

        there will be nothing
          but my beautiful skeleton
           floating in a pool,
            all the discs and vertebrae
           moving perfectly; nothing but
          a spine moving
         in an undulating dance,
        constant and graceful;
       nothing but a skeleton,
      my skeleton:
       a fluid X-ray of
        an Alvin Ailey dancer whirls
          arches, jumps, tumbles — a spine
            moving perfectly to shining choreography.

Menopause

Sitting in their darkening
gardens, women begin
to cackle & damn. *The cosmos is*

slipping down a black hole,
one mentions, *while the doctor*
offers chirpy little pamphlets.

Another tried
to communicate to her
dumbstruck husband:

The world is
a very bleak place
without estrogen.

Except, they laugh,
for us, the ladies
eating filbert brittle,

knitting cruelty and
kindness in the
seed-blasted gardens.

Autumn in the New Century

stood ready to stride in,
with stiletto heels,
"total ownership" of an A-line skirt,
shades of jalapeño and mustard,
comfortable classics. All the rage:
exotic cheese, heads of unusual
lettuce, fashions celebrating
tribalism, and tattoos too. Everyone wanted
a shorter commute.

               Instead, autumn fell
in shades of ash, soot, disfigured,
heels over head, the entrepreneurial
economy in suspended animation. It came
with slashed payrolls, empty
airports. It came with wailing and silence.
No one would invest in a kite factory.

Autumn came wrenched with twisted
buildings, body parts, thoughts
of gas masks, flat-heeled boots
for evacuation, pantsuits
for crawling under, knee-jerk anger,
and caution. It came with eyes
squeezed or streaming, wearing
videos of thousands of funerals,
donating blood, holding orphans,
and waving a multitude of flags.

The Live-In

I'd been beaten down by psychopaths and needed to get in touch with my inner harpy. Call me crazy, but I decided to adopt a real one, sent paperwork to Strophades where they live. I was surprised when she arrived in a cage, snarling and whining, because she had my face, most disconcerting, or was it my mother's? Her body, of course, was that of a predatory bird. For thirteen weeks I took her everywhere, enjoying the startled looks, the careful respect with which men greeted us. Women stared, shook their heads, and departed.

At church, the minister straightened his tie, nodded at me, and talked of self-respect and God. My harpy shrieked through the hymns and ushers asked us to leave. Oddly, she had difficulty eating steak and Oysters Rockefeller, preferred table scraps and junk food. Her stench was stunning. She stole shiny objects for her cage, and our poor dog growled and whimpered through her stay.

I learned from her claws—how to sink talons in and shred, and from her wings—how at dusk when I left the cage open, she soared over tree tops, diving to snatch rodent and bird carcasses. For the dog's sake, I sent her back, but I miss how she helped dry the dishes at night while shrieking for blood and carrion, and how she pulled up my pants with her beak after she broke my arm. I swear she cackled and blew me a kiss.

Queen Gluttony to Her Confessor

These are some of my vices:
sleeping late, over-eating,
carelessness about status,
mind-hunger so great
I devour books,
leaving their broken-backed
carcasses throughout my lair.
Hatred of — and boredom with —
a lot of small talk, whimsy
at inappropriate times,
spoiling my dog with bones
and cookies. Hanging out
with my twisted sister-pal, Wrath.
She specializes in anger,
the kind that makes mountains
tremble, makes tsunamis level villages.

But back to me and my vices.
A greater love of trees and plants,
especially those that bear fruit,
than of many human beings.
A horror of human foibles,
of human stupidity, including
my own. An ability to stare at
ocean waves for hours, my eyes
drinking in the surf like wine.
An inability to digest
pomposity. Reckless courage
when something scrumptious
is involved. A failure to
bow and scrape. After a feast,
my loud laugh – too loud,
but in the right places.

My Favorite Incarnations

A tidal pool,
an eagle's nest,
a small green snake
slithering among the reeds.

Once I was a flying horse,
a friend of Pegasus.
Another time, a painter of tiles
in an ancient Italian villa.
I loved soaring,
       a snowy owl,
over winter forests, and
the long stationary life—
a stately Douglas Fir.

There were painful ones,
with cockroaches and rapists,
but I'd rather remember

that happy, slender woman,
long ago, looking out
at the brilliant Greek sea
while lazily eating
figs and dates—
an exotic dancer who had
caught the eye of Alexander.

Now I'm a breeze
whispering *through*
swaying cedars,
a song you can't quite
remember, sad and funny,
punctuated by whistle,
waterfall, and chimes.

Smitten with a Different Television

Screens flash everywhere—TVs, laptops, iMacs,
iPads, smartphones. Husband sits in front of
three screens, multiple windows open, screens
within screens, while he scrolls and talks
on two phones, laughing. Gamer daughter
kills expertly in full-color 3D space, her avatar,
in body armor with machine gun and crossbow,
shoots endlessly, explosion upon explosion,
as she mutters to her remote, raiding squadron,
scattered across the country, through her headset.
I close their doors.

When we were children, my older sister caught
me sitting cross-legged on the floor
staring at our black-and-white television,
which was off. She told my mother I was strange,
but Mother, folding the endless laundry while staring
out the window, retorted, "Nonsense. Daydreaming
runs in the family." Sunlight finger-painted
the huge green maple leaves out my bedroom
window. I stared for hours at trees and sky,
white cumulus clouds shaped like wooly caterpillars
or schooners or griffins drifting slowly,
the smell of frying bacon wafting upward.

I was a tiny explorer walking
on my ceiling, the whole house turned
topsy-turvy. The maples waved
at me and later my friends and I
biked all over town, threw water balloons
at boys we liked. Television was for when
you were tired, at night. It was like
staring into a fire on the hearth, where
shapes from another world
glowed and crackled and smoldered.

To Visit with the Grape Hyacinth

Others laugh, but I know
to look at small things.

I jump from my car
to observe

green blade-like leaves,
miniature stalks leading

to clumps of upside down
grape clusters.

Tiny bluish purplish
flowers, each opening

edged in white.
Like dappled, purple

kisses. For a moment
I cease acting
like I will live forever.

Tree Music

Just buds on the aspens now,
but by summer
not only a shimmer of leaves
but a murmur

will swell on the high plains
where ancient trees
were clear cut, silenced, and now
protected young groves,

silver and green cloisonné,
prepare to tune up,
rustle a subtle, percussive
song that we will miss

unless we stand on one foot
like the Great Horned
Owl, rotate our heads perfectly,
and become still—listen.

Spell of Enchantment

An owl has grabbed a rabbit again.
Blackbirds in my crock-pot beg
to be baked in a pie.
In the fireplace a fox curls, sleeping.
Too soon, too soon, my old friends
turn up dead —
disease, suicide, accident.
Today they pulled
a friend's body
out of a river
and then the telephone rang
and I called
people I never call
to let them know
an owl has grabbed another
rabbit. In the fireplace
a fox curls, sleeping.
One woman whispered,
"It's terrible that this
is what makes us
call each other, that death
casts a spell of enchantment."
Blackbirds in my crock-pot
beg to be baked in a pie.
We wonder which friends will
live into old age,
and if we will be among them.
Today, my mother who has
outlasted her husband,
all her younger siblings,
and most of her friends,
understands my need to talk:
"Too soon, too soon,
 old friends turn up dead."
Another owl grabs another rabbit,
always.

Brazen Hussy

I'm not sorry for the pumpernickel smell rising
from the cafés of St. Petersburg where we
strolled in fur-lined hats and boots, our
long legs stamping the snow as we hooted
into foreign air. I'm not sorry at all.

Women are taught to be sorry —
sorry they're bright, take up room, exist. I'm a threat
because I loved it — accepting rancid lovers on a whim
or turning others down like a prim maiden aunt,
dancing on tables in Moscow, walking the long way home
in Frisco, making lots of money in pinstripe suits,

and now blessedly staying home,
hunkered down in the house to tell racy stories.
Radical housewives are the supreme threat.
I'm not sorry that I've survived, while friends —
I keep being notified — are dying. I have discovered
the pleasures of eating exotic olives standing in my
kitchen and rubbing the belly of a handsome dog.

If we live our lives being sorry and crooked, we
are rotting leaves in place of a newborn calf, burnt
toast instead of wet pine needles on the forest floor,
the halitosis of rejected nuns when we could be
lavender wands waved by witch-girls on May Day.

Stone Heart

After, you got in your blue Toyota,
drove home to your husband,
careful not to run stop signs,
not to pass in no passing zones.
Filthy drunk from the office
party, tears dried on your face.
You'd driven round for hours with
your lover, the father you'd never known,
who ordered you to throw empties
out the car window in case of cops.
Before you got out of his gold Mercedes,
the car you made fun of,
you climbed into his lap,
desperate hooked fish. He slid
the sun roof open, laughing,
now you knew what sun roofs
were for, fucking the rest stop
in darkness, the best part
the cool night air on your head,
which bobbed like a jill-in-the-box
on speed, laughter turned to weeping
on his upturned face, his look of
surrender, eyes closed. You liked
to do it in truck stops, cheap motels.
You loved to feel like scum, hated yourself,
loved the coming and going,
the driving home alone, barely
remembering to turn on headlights,
to yield as you turned onto separate
highways, the radio turned up loud,
Mick Jagger & The Rolling Stones
screaming, "You can never
break, never break, never break
this heart of stone."

Never

> *After a story about a girl who
> was forbidden to touch her doll*

There is only one way to burn that box.
My mother told me never to take the doll
out of the box, never to comb its hair,
"because you don't know how to take care of her."

From the hospital, thirty-five years later, I asked
her to send me the doll. My hand shook holding
the telephone. My voice quavered like a little girl's.
She relented, told me again, never to take the doll

out of the box, never to comb its hair,
"because you still don't know how to take care of her."
The doll arrived at my home. I took her
out of the box. *I did not comb her hair.*

I put her in a chair. My husband told me
not to burn the box in anger, to wait
till I knew what I was doing.
And, I have done nothing. Gunshot can come

from the top of any tall building
if you dare to walk the streets.
How can I raise a comb to that small head,
stroke the forbidden hair?

First, I would have to put my mother
in that box, nail tight the cover,
then light the kindling under that coffin,
while the little girl in her chair

stares at the flames licking the cardboard,
curling its edges to black ash.
I'd chant the words I'm too scared to say:
I give birth to myself now that you are dead.

My First Job

Over steaming pots, the cooks were ornery,
flushed. In uniforms and hairnets, we constantly
scuttled — placing orders, delivering food. The boss

with pursed lips often screamed. Those first weeks,
at night I'd collapse on my schoolgirl bed, my arms, legs,
back all ached. A few times I cried. Early on, I had trouble

remembering, brought the wrong dish, apologized.
A customer snapped, "This soup is cold. Take it back."
"Yes, ma'am," I replied and lifted the hot bowl. I can still

see the steam rising from that fragrant chowder.
Some people were kind, though they didn't have to be.
Soft, gentle words and smiles. Origami birds and coins.

During lulls I read Plato's Republic and studied
an aging redhead who spat: "Yaw just heah for the
summah. Ya don't know what this life is like.

I raised my baby in a cahdbawd box,
couldn't affawd a crib." At sixteen, I served all kinds,
learned to swallow the good with the bad.

After a while, I hit my stride. At the end of each day,
I poured a heap of tips onto my bureau,
breezed out to the movies or on a date.

Decades later, when my brother-in-law barked at a young
waitress in a little café, I wanted to climb under the table.
Plato understood: *A petty tyrant beholding his own*

soul may behave unrighteously and deteriorates his lot.
The waitress didn't get angry; she just brought the order.
You learn a lot bringing food to people.

Russian Roulette

Each the youngest of four,
my husband and I both
had mothers who
told us we were "mistakes."

They'd giggle and add,
"Well, an afterthought," (his)
or "I was playing Russian Roulette
with my diaphragm,

if you know what I mean." (mine)
My mother described
her labor to me: "It was
The Fifties. The doctor sat on

my hospital bed and pleaded,
'Take something for the pain.
I wouldn't let my wife do this!'
I said no, this is my fourth,

and I want to remember,
so *I never do this again.*"
After hearing this story
five times, I asked,

"What was it like — labor, I mean?"
"You go into shock the pain's so great,"
she said matter-of-factly, "sort of like
breaking a leg." That's all she said.

My husband's mother, demure and coy,
but just as sly, would often go on,
as my husband squirmed,
"Oh, he was a real *surprise*, you know.

Have no idea how it happened,
after six years. Found him
under a cabbage leaf.
Fairies must have brought him."

They say opposites attract
and drive each other crazy.
We clash and we thrash
and sing of grit & whimsy.

Inheritance

I do not want it,
the cackling laugh,
the satiric turn of phrase,
old as the Irish washerwomen
coming home from the laundries.

I do not want it,
the ability to see the weakness
in every argument,
the penetrating gaze,
ancient as the Germanic lawyers
jousting in the courts of Europe.

I do not want it,
sensing what others cannot sense,
the anguish of someone's
past or future, the moment I enter
a room and know something's wrong,
like a ragtag Bohemian gypsy ridiculed
along her caravan route.

I do not want them,
the crystal ball, the law book,
the laundry basket,
yet they are mine.

Before Our Minister's Child Rape Trial, We Visit a Voodoo Priest in New Orleans

How kind the "witch doctor" was!
He said we had to pray
for *justice with love*,
not for evil, never for evil.
Past the sequined flags,
sacred bottles, we sat. No black candles,
no hexes, no incantations. We held
hands with him and bowed as if to pray,
not to some pathetic
patriarch, glorified clerk,
who won't lift a finger to stop
priests & ministers ramming
mouths, vaginas & anuses
of girls & boys

but to the earth and all her spirits —
animal & plant & water —
Ogoun, warrior loa, Damballah, serpent loa, Erzulie,
mermaid loa of love, protect us, spirits,
fill us with your power
while we stick our necks out,
we cannot pray to God now, maybe never,
our betrayal is too complete.
Afterward, the voodoo priest
gave me four red *gris-gris* pouches,
filled with herbal potions & wood shavings,
that he claimed, were from the chair of
the long-dead Voodoo Queen,
mulatto hairdresser Marie Laveau —
pouches for me as a witness and for
the raped girls of color,
pouches to protect us during the trial.

At the Court House,
holding my head up,
in a white linen suit,
fingering the red pouch
in my pocket, *please come through,*
oh criminal justice system,
I sat next to the small
dark-skinned girls
and our bodyguard, a surprise,
furnished by a concerned lawyer,
as white men & women churchgoers

scowled, looked away, turned their backs,
openly shunning me

(Hadn't we been friends? Hadn't the minister
been my friend? Madame Laveau urged
in a dream: *Sometimes a male dog like this
must be put in a cage. It's the only way to stop him.*)
because of my crime—
the audacity I'd shown turning him in,
a woman bringing worms to the surface.
*And I thought racism was a thing
of the past. What a dumbass white
bitch I was.* I remembered

how the policeman
stood questioningly
in my front doorway
and served
my rape trial subpoena:
witness for the prosecution.
"I've been dreading
this day. My minister,
he did things to girls,"
I stammered,
and the young
police officer's
honor, my shock,
as he faced me
with respect
and replied, "Ma'am,
sometimes we must do
these things
to get rid of
the vermin."
But my minister
was *a man*, like other men,
good and evil terribly
intertwined. We can only do
what we think is right,
no matter the price,
so we'll have
no regrets,
and hope
the good spirits,
this time,
prevail.

Amethyst

Like her fine desert watercolors—
lilac-colored skies
on tiny paper swatches,
the new ring on my finger
changes my mind.

A woman with elfin eyes
like a European figurine, she
told me she found her son,
my husband, under a cabbage leaf.
The perfect stitches of her dolls
and doll clothes amaze me, and
her furnished dollhouse rooms,
acres of cloth, beads, and sequins
she turns into children's toys—
puppets, animals, ornaments.
At eighty years of age,
she gives me the amethyst,
an old family ring she takes off her finger.

I'd kept my maiden name.
Now I write her:
for our twentieth anniversary
I will change my last name to hers.

When I see Vidalia onions
at the Farmer's Market, I ship a box to her—
a woman who could live on
onion sandwiches, a woman
who says, "Every day is Mother's day."
When her husband sat strapped up,
brain-dead from Alzheimer's,
like some god's huge and ghastly puppet,
I told her I loved her.
She sobbed, "It's so hard to let go."
I knew this death was authentic,
just like elves, dollhouses,
a fat baby under a cabbage leaf,
like this delicate, purple-violet
which makes me a member of her clan.

Taking a Spin with Voltaire

What thoughts I have tonight, Voltaire,
as I watch the news, peruse the internet.
How did you invent
your half-assed hero
in the "best of all possible worlds"?
What exquisite pain drove you
to planetary satire? Volcanoes still
erupt, priests rape, earthquakes swallow
civilizations, soldiers kill because
infantile rulers give them orders.

How timeless, how inappropriate!
Voltaire, I would like
to serve you a meal:
fresh salmon grilled by my
husband, asparagus steamed to
perfection by me. We will honor
you rather than send you to
the Bastille. We'll show you
huge rhododendron flowers,
raise goblets of organic pinot noir.

We'll dance, my husband and I,
and you with your brilliant
mistress, Marquise du Châtelet, twirling
and twirling over
the cedar decks while neighbors
stare and gasp through their binoculars.
What did you try
to do with your life, Voltaire?
Bring people to reason through

humor or tear down the state
with anger? Try this sourdough
bread and fresh butter. Try these
blackberries baked in a crust.
Enjoy the giant Douglas firs;
drink more pinot noir! I wander through
real and virtual worlds, Voltaire,
looking for you and your rapier
wit, a term that now has been
ruined by half-assed, gawky
pseudo-intellectuals who've
never held a sword!

We're poisoning oceans, warming the air.
People still kill each other over religion,
but the weapons are beyond big.
What work would you pick now?
Would you blog and tend organics?
Hey, Voltaire, try this striped zucchini
I grew. Tell me about your chestnut trees
and vegetables at Ferney, your green estate—
the intellectual capital of Europe! Then
dance with me under the cedars
while Anna's Hummingbirds fly above us,
planets and galaxies spin.
What should we do with our lives?

The Swan Boats

        glide silently
            where willows
                hang their hair
                    into the lake
                        on Boston Common.
                            A chubby little girl yearns
                    for that wordless
              grace, quiet and kind.
          Her shiny black
     patent leather shoes
blister her feet.
      Grandmother talks,
           where willows
                hang their hair,
                    endless adult talk.
                        At the lake on
                            Boston Common,
                      the boats shaped like
              swans
                  float
                        on lighted ripples.
                  Nothing else
              in her life
            makes her feel
              like the swan boats
                  gliding, where willows
                        hang their hair.

OMG, Emily's on Facebook!

Some inspect the shallows,
far fewer seek the Deep—
there are no Ruts to follow—
no map, no key, no creed.

Technology – always seething.
Epiphany? Impromptu—
a Friend – Within – is breathing—
our task – a Rendezvous –

Sylvia Plath at 75

She didn't kill herself, you see.
She told Ted he was a *stinking varmint*,
summoning her gutsy American
colloquial speech, took the kids
back to bonny *New* England,
and immediately got a teaching job
at Radcliffe, soon to be merged
with Harvard. Her writing came
to life, rather than to death, and
she managed to burn all her journals
before they were published.
She turned away from the notion that
a woman perfected is a dead woman,
and she earned herself many friends
and worthy enemies, enemies she
could be proud of. Now wrinkled,
75 years old, and happily married
to a stable non-poet,
she lounges with Maxine and Anne,
who finally managed
to get on meds and kick the liquor,
at Maxine's farm, and reminisces
about the old days —
how crazy Anne and Sylvia
had been for self-immolation
and victim metaphors, how their
own bootstraps saved them.
She marvels at how they've
earned their Pulitzers and are
still around to irritate those
who hate successful women.

Stiff Gin & Tonics

My pilot father flew The Hump
during World War II, holed up
briefly in northern India
with British officers who drank
stiff gin and tonics all day
to defeat their tropical fevers,
as did he, who didn't even
make it to the Taj Mahal.

I also love wild juniper berries,
grains, botanicals, spring water,
and spirits filtered through
crushed volcanic rock—
extraordinary Essence
of Genièvre (juniper),
a concoction from Holland
(according to gin historians),
later adopted by Brits
after William of Orange, the Protestant,
assumed the throne,
and curbed imports of Roman Catholic
wine. More and more was consumed;
even Quakers in The Colonies
drank gin after funerals.

In the imperial tropics,
the English mixed gin
with quinine, their treatment
for malaria. Churchill believed fervently
in the drink. Served a sweet Tom Collins,
Winston spat it out. Churchill proclaimed,
"The gin and tonic has saved
more Englishmen's lives, and minds,
than all the doctors in the Empire."

My father kept a list of pilots
he'd trained with, crossed out
names when they died. Threw out
the list when most names
had a line through them. He wrote my
mother, "It would be fast. I figure I'd see red,

and be gone." He once admitted in the late sixties,
"I think we smoked pot or hashish with a raj,
but really I can't remember
because of gin."

I raise a glass of Essence of Juniper
made in Bend, Oregon,
with tonic and a twist of lime,
glass glinting in sunlight,
to Churchill and to my dead father.
The tang of lime and quinine – their wit,
the fragrance of desert juniper – their longing.

The Prize

After astonishing & harrowing travels
through foreign lands—blood sports,
saffron & peppers, masquerades,
tropical fevers, naked & draped bodies,
whispers, shouts in guttural patois—

the Learned One arrives in a sequestered,
familiar place where the local tribe (his)
asks few questions, eats bland gruel.
Soon, he yearns to drink high-proof,
exotic brandy in this land of piss-water.

Uniqueness had never been his plan.
Supreme curiosity, care, effort
have sentenced him to this escape.
Like a blind man in a cell
slowly realizing he's entombed,

an epiphany takes hold:
wherever he roams, he's in exile,
even at home.

Iphigenia, Coming On Fast

It was my very last Lucy in the Sky routine.
Grass grew thirty-feet high. I was a worm.
(Father had phoned that he must *please the gods*.)
Only my death could change the wind? I cowered,
waiting for a monster-movie-sized bird
to peck me dead. Everything came down
to blood. I asked a tiny floating college boy,
"What's this stuff do to your brain anyway?"

I felt staccato — why should I be sacrificed
so troops could sail for Troy? I began to crawl
across the field to my dorm room where
students sat bored with birth control pills &
Dostoevsky. My white dress fluttered
as I looked into unloving Father's face —
a field of dead grass. Did he even have
a decent *theory*? It was time for me to travel,
geographically. A thousand ships could wait.

Paleolithic Crone:
The Beginning of Craft

Spirited Woman With Four Arms
under a starving moon,
spirit wearing green,
I grew up in a tree.
Skeletons spooked me.
I learned to make love
to my own fear,
and to paint all I see.
A new mouth opened
to deep caverns
of one-thousand paintings.
I walk the sands
with my holy stick,
draw the dance of stars, sky,
the night glow emerging
from clouds like mammoths.

Spirited Woman With Four Arms
draws on the cave walls —
beasts and hunters,
breasts and babies,
blood and spears.
After I show others
how to paint the spirits,
animals start to come
to me. Wolverines lie down
at my feet. The young
come to watch. Keeper
of one thousand paintings,
I keep watch over my clan.
My hands are strong with spirit.
I know the colors
of berries, dirts, and roots.

Blue Kayak

Liquid liberation—
those trips alone, just the river and trees.
Bluebirds near the water sang freedom
to the periwinkle, and you,
beautiful you, could feel something,
not just numb—one with the ultramarine
river in your kayak, escaping
cocktails with society.

Self-possessed, you paddled alone,
down a narrower and narrower path
to a death
I could never have foreseen,
though there were signs,
always signs,
and sadness gripped you
even at sixteen.

I thought you stronger than I, shining,
a woman I would rejoin later,
in mirth and song. I remember you in
youth swimming in the sun in my
hometown, the only one
who could swim
farther than I.
Those midsummer days,

I'll never forget how we breast stroked
across the aqua lake,
the azure sky and cumulus clouds reflected
in its surface.
We were very tall girls, statuesque—
a male friend says we took
his breath away.

Once in June heat a group of girls came
upon a cool, cobalt river.
You shed your clothes,
boldly tumbled in
to refresh your body.
We others followed you,

disrobed, were
water nymphs to your Diana,
before the awestruck crowd.

The Headmaster—shocked
by reports of skinny-dipping—
never would have believed
the shy, quiet girl
had led the others on.

Could you foresee the search
helicopters, the front page splash
when you left the shore
for the last time?

Friend, how could you
drown in middle age?
The best swimmer I ever loved.
Why did you take
what we liked best
and make it into a weapon,
an indigo shroud,
your final oblivion?

Poem Written in a Copy of *The Aeneid*

At times I've asked myself what madness
made me crawl into the hide of a dead language,
attempt to follow the path of a warrior, courage
and fatalism combined. My first iambs, anapests.
Five years I sat before the texts of Caesar, Horace, Virgil.
At ancient wooden desks, thick books and Cassell's—
that wondrous dictionary. We studied meter, heroic tales,
humbled ourselves before the generous Miss DeMille,
who with patience and a smile taught us well—
to mind every quirk, every case and conjugation,
and the philosophy that seeped from this citadel—
although *omnes una manet nox*, humans seek to build
monuments, cities, governments, art, invention.
Despite constant misfortune, a few are fulfilled.

"*Omnes una manet nox*" - *The same night awaits us all*. (Horace)

When We Were Flying Fish

Once I asked myself, when was I happy?
I stood in a lonely doorway with a
hickory broom. The baby upchucked
on the floor. Mops and sponges
were next, down on my hands and knees.
I'd traded a briefcase and heels for this —
black skillets encrusted, diaper stench,
windows stuck on a winter sky.

When was I happy?
I was pretending to fly,
my arms spread like eagle wings.
Over and over I soared,
laughing down into ocean foam
in summer sun and rose up smiling
at your handsome tan bearded face.
We were not yet a pair.

To fly over the houses, to join
the swallows, sparrows, crows.
To alight in the top branches and look
down on the tiny people and tiny crises.
Then look up to clouds drifting over
a thumbnail moon.

Even the salt in my mouth wonderful,
the smell of your skin,
the impossible green of the ocean,
the never ending surf —
you held the small of my back
as I floated with my eyes closed,
and I knew.

Couple with Ginger Lilies

A blind man falls in love with a woman with no arms.
He marries her mellifluous voice describing cathedrals,
perennial gardens, smorgasbords he'll never see.

Years later, trying to describe an impressionist painting,
she feels trapped in a tarantella. That night he dreams
of a wife who can hug him back, arms wrapped tightly

round his torso. The woman practices erotic maneuvers
with her legs, mouth. The man starts singing arias.
Together they begin gourmet cooking, the wife reciting recipes,

guiding the husband's hands to rosemary, coriander jars,
with her voice. Still, they drift apart, floating like lonely
Chagall creatures. The blind man misses her Chartres,

she finds no one to hold her. Proud, they persist in their
middle-age self-improvement programs, he exploring
Austrian opera, she admiring Martinique bougainvillea.

They meet for drinks. She finds herself regaling him
with a faraway land where all the women cradle men
in muscular, brown legs. The man buys ginger lilies,

holds them for her to sniff. Their hearts flutter, rise
like Gregorian chants or steaming ratatouille,
buzz like hummingbirds into drooping fuchsia flowers.

Half a Valentine for Mister Wonderful

        You're my
        dessert, Mister
        Richer-than-God.
        I'm your bottle girl—
        bring cold Heinekens,
        wear nothing but
        dark glasses. Whisper,
        "Let's just lie in bed
        and talk all night."
        Growl, "You're
        perfect just
        the way
        you
        are."

                                                                                         Mister
I'm your cow-tongued buttered bun,   Windy
                                                                                     Wallets.

            Slay me!

Dominatrix Month-by-Month Planner

Jan:	Moon for tying executives to their desks, cracking my whip.

Feb:	Valentine with handcuffs, thick leather belt moon.

Mar:	Moon of muddy Great Dane feet mounting you.

Apr:	Pulleys and ladders moon, water buckets & D-rings.

May:	Wrist and ankle restraints, worm your way to flower bud moon.

Jun:	Moon of mandatory listening, blindfolded, to baby birds.

Jul:	Silent moon with surprise fireworks behind your eyelids.

Aug:	Run through garden sprinklers or else moon.

Sep:	School bus fantasy moon or ruler to your knuckles.

Oct:	Naughty Jack O'Lantern, crawl, my darling.

Nov:	Moon of sitting on you, feeding you turkey & cranberry.

Dec:	Garters and stockings under my fur coat, you'll beg among the icicles.

    Now tell me when
    to pencil you in.

The Tyranny of Women

- ✓ Elaborate protocols of apology.

- ✓ Interminable frilly conversation about handbags, glitter hags, hair-dos.

- ✓ Felicity describes how she lost her virginity in an old Ford in clinical detail though we definitely didn't ask.

- ✓ Sycophantic ones in miniskirts, Deanna and Debbie, giggling and sucking up to the only guy in the room.

- ✓ Bizarre stories of laundry compulsions by Eleanor though we're clearly not interested.

- ✓ Katy frequents sex chat rooms while her toddler sits for hours in front of the TV.

- ✓ Susie often gets us to change meetings to fit her schedule and then never shows up.

- ✓ Stiletto heels and suit, "kick down, kiss up," Stephanie is rising through the corporation.

- ✓ Melanie is spreading negative rumors about a certain woman we all know.

- ✓ A dynamic one, Helen organizes female "self-esteem" groups while her son vandalizes the neighborhood.

- ✓ Mirabelle is mentally dragging her abusive mother around with her, like tying a decaying horse to your leg, and we're all supposed to be sympathetic.

- ✓ Bambi, though she's a geophysicist and belly dancer, brings tears to her eyes, in the discussion group, whenever she feels attention has drifted a bit too far from me, myself, and I.

- ✓ All that I'm not supposed to say.

- ✓ My husband says the men aren't any better.

Trumpet Flower Vine in August

Shooting out long tendrils of green daily,
I curl round your pergola,
beautiful and monstrous,
no curfew for my growing,
and on to the roof of your house.

With clusters of orange-red buds,
I trumpet
joy joy joy   to the bees,
buzzing, intoxicated
by my plethora of pollen.

Hidden in flickering
light, high on my branches,
squirrels chatter and nest.
Sun-drenched afternoons,
hummingbirds hover
before my tapered
rosy champagne flutes,
their flight so ephemeral
you stop,
               mid-sentence,
and point.

               I could eat
your house with abandon!
Listen to my symphony —
dappled shadows,
gaudy happiness —
and take heart.
You too can prosper.

Ars Poetica: A Charm of Hummingbirds

They evolved

>> to pollinate thousands
>>> of plant species
>>>> as they dine on nectar.
> Their bladed beaks fit
>> bright blooms —
> purple, magenta, ruby tubes —
>> tiny keys in tiny locks
>>> all over the Americas.

Wide-open jaws
> catch insects
>> with deadly accuracy
> while flying.

>> Unlike
> other birds' wings,
> theirs move deftly

backwards,

>>>> forwards,

> and figure eights.

The only birds that can

>>>> hover

> they make intricate dances
>> from a limited repertoire
> of movements —

captivating acrobatics,
> visits to a thousand flowers
>> between dawn and dusk,
> and at the bottom
>> of their mating dives,

                a chirp
                        produced by
                                spreading
                                        iridescent tail feathers.

Their hearts beat
        600 times a minute,
                as they dive-bomb
                        to glory.

Purple-throated,
        ruby-throated,
                fire-crowned,
                        they migrate
        thousands of miles
according to season.

In their varied nests—
        just
                        two tiny eggs

                and silence.

Hiking in the Sonoran Desert

Cacti make certain you don't forget
not to touch next time. Not touch
or even brush, so fragile
they must be spike-covered.
Much can survive amid harshness,
like some of us. What's one trick?
Become a canteen —
night-blooming cereus stores
so much water its tuber may weigh
more than a toddler.
Develop prickles
so no one can eat you.
Or reduce your leaves
to pinhead size, coat them with wax,
or hairy mats. Mesquite
fold their leaves
on hot days, while jojoba
angle their leaves
edgewise to the sun's mid-day rays.
No rain, and ocotillo stand bare
like clusters of buggy whips.
Many of us have long shallow rootlets
through earth's uppermost layers
where there's moisture.
We can lie dormant for years,
waiting for our green chance.
But I'm tired of this visit
in unforgiving terrain,
a way of life I left years ago.
I long for affection,
a soothing, giant rhododendron
in bloom, vegetable caresses
and mist in the Northwest.
I sway in the merciless heat.

Mona Lisa Discusses Money

Mio Dio, you think it was easy being a vixen
on stage, smiling for Leonardo? My husband, a fop—
querulous, hovering, worried the painter was far
shabbier than we knew, that he'd paint a tart—
unseemly for our social class. His lexicon omitted love
with its messy contradictions; I was his ox,
young, genteel, yes, but never talked to, no fizz
allowed, no impromptu dancing. I had to bob,
calypso-dance in secret, sell embroidery. I did
everything to keep us afloat, modeled as if
granting Leonardo a favor, but, sophisticated man,
I didn't have to tell him except with my eyes: luck
knocked not at our door. He gave me coins; I lit up the room.

Impossibly Huge Female

She loomed like a skyscraper among village huts,
like a sequoia among juniper bushes. She was
fat, wore empire-waist polyester dresses from
the Half Size Department, where her mother took her,
babbling banalities in the car. Boys came up to her chest
at dancing school, and held her white-gloved hands.
"Hi, Jolly Green Giant!" "Hi, Empire State Building!"
Her mother took her downtown, through underground
hospital corridors, to the Growth Doctor, his waiting room
full of tiny boys and giant girls. Waiting, she remembered
her father had said she'd end in the circus, said it and
laughed, so she'd guessed it was funny. No one looked at
anyone else in the waiting room, and she couldn't imagine
how they could expand those tiny boys...
Measured and weighed, weighed and measured,
her monthly height plotted on charts. The tall male
Growth Doctor hesitated to give her the hormone pills;
her height was "already beginning to plateau."
Mother asked her if she wanted to take the pills.
She felt like an alien dropped from space,
but she didn't know that had nothing to do with her height.
Her mother loudly on the phone: *How she'll find a husband,
I'll never know.* She said yes. She would have said yes
to anything, anything that might shut up her mother.
After all was done, the Growth Doctor announced,
they might have shaved a quarter inch.
By high school, she was a statuesque knockout,
but she never felt like one. She had girlfriends who were taller,
who'd never visited Growth Doctors. Some had parents
who said, "It's wonderful being tall. You'll see."
Twenty years later, she wanted that quarter-inch back.
She wanted a mother and father who loved her
just the way she was. She practiced growing
gargantuan and finally joined the circus. She became
The Woman Who Dares To Take Up Space.

Because of Ouspensky

They were rapping at a coffeehouse, *The Idler*.
Cambridge, Massachusetts. 1960s. People were into
macrobiotics, Indian bedspreads, anti-war protests,
hash pipes, Marxism, "the pill." The abolition of
private property. He followed her,
tall blonde in faded jeans, out the door,
quoting whole passages from Norman O. Brown.
Cobble-stoned street corner in summer heat,
cannabis-scented night air. A radio blasted
Bob Dylan singing "Sad-Eyed Lady of the Lowlands."
They talked altered states of consciousness, origin of
the universe, "peak" experiences. She said O.K.
In the bedroom of his graduate student apartment,
past the books on cement blocks, they took off
their clothes. He said, "Nothing's going to happen
unless you want it to happen. *The body itself
is a mind-altering substance.*"

                                          Harvard Square
was on fire at midnight as she walked,
connected to the sky, the lights,
the streets, the stars, everything vibrating.

Kept

The eyelids   a giant movie screen
   falling slowly into
        the pleasures of
    brocade   taffeta
like Madame Bovary   would have desired.
   It's been so long   since I allowed myself
     the pleasure of touching   fabric
    staring at colors   one wants to roll in.
The beautiful young
   Portuguese woman   at work
    began to talk about   loving to smell
      different perfumes   at the store counter —
   she listed
     fragrance after fragrance
I'd never whiffed.
No one had ever   lifted
   glass bottles to my nose   whispered
      "Smell this and this."   Feminine pleasures, why
    should they be   denied?   Languor
and silk   in secluded boudoirs
   are calling.   Always there are
  foreign furnishings   pungent aromas   the plush
      of tassled pillows   a green-eyed cat
        stretching.

Locked-Up Girls

Wolf, swan, koala bear,
flamingo, black panther—
you each choose
an animal to be.
You will write
what you smell,
see, taste, hear, touch,
and do
as this animal
in the class I teach
within walls
that lock you in.
Your eyes deep,
somber, dark, sweet,
or so vacant
I worry that the spirit
has already left your body.
Your mothers are dead
or drug addicts, all of you
violated, or even shot-up
with drugs as babies
to shut-you-up.
You've been runaways,
prostitutes, stabbers,
and yet—you're
beautiful, smart,
tattoos snaking up
your arms, or rings
piercing your lips,
or your eyes like
a seventy-year-old woman's.
Some judge sent you here
to help you,
but you'll be sent back
to some hell hole of a home.
I try to create a space for you
to imagine   your   self
as a wild animal—
capable, strong, free.

Astro-Girl! or, I've Been Reading Manga

Stronger than every boy,
she kicks — KE-BOOM!
with steel-tipped boots.
Her hair, purple & black
stripes. A flying phoenix
tattoo spirals her left bicep.
With bustier of reclaimed
pheasant feathers & fur,
thick silver belt, she
murmurs hexes and
sprouts wings.
She's quick — KA-BAMMM!
rising into the sky, then down
to kick again.

In the alley, behind a bar,
supporters are watching her
Kung Fu moves
on a blubbering dude
down on his knees
who thought he could show
his fabulous power over
all things female. Only one
problem, pal, she's been
practicing on Marines.
You can't touch her!

She could care less about your
fragile male ego, deflating now –
SHWISH SHWUSH –
your need to prove how
on top you are,
and she thinks you should
get a life,
leave girls alone, and if you're
lucky – DUH – doubtful! –
the guys lounging in the corner, jeering,
might pull her away,
so you can reconstruct
a personality from rubble,
realizing — too late — that she
could have been your
avenging angel – POW POW!
as she soars away.

Thirteen Noir Tweets

(1) He woke on the floor on a dirty dog bed. He looked at his body and saw fur. He barked and jumped around. Shit! What was in those drinks?

(2) At the big bachelorette party, she opened the last gift. A dozen black silk roses and a card: "You bitch. He's still mine."

(3) "Why did you always treat me like there was something wrong with me?" he implored. His mother sneered, "You're just like your father."

(4) In her aunt's ancient diary she found the following passage about herself: "It's better that she doesn't know I'm her mother."

(5) He caressed her black silk stockings, whispered, "What animal do you like to pretend to be?" She handcuffed him, replied, "Black widow."

(6) At dawn, in her bathrobe, she phoned 911. A corpse sprawled across her front porch. "No, I don't know him and I'm not a morning person!"

(7) A wave washed a body up on a beach. Not a real beach, nor a real wave. He awoke screaming, under a dead man.

(8) "I bought killer black sandals to wear with my evening gown," she told her friend. "This time I'll remember to pack my Smith & Wesson."

(9) At twilight he sat in a rocker on the porch waiting for her to come home. He'd found their love notes. Rocking, with a pistol in his lap.

(10) "No divorce," she thought, eyes like slits, staring at his botched grout-and-tile project. Rather, she'd go on a Greek cruise, as a widow.

(11) His fiftieth birthday party — crack cocaine with a lady of the night. He dropped dead. What a way for the high school basketball coach to go.

(12) "What a glorious day," he thought, floating in a hot air balloon over a bay where he'd soon jettison a burlap bag shaped like his wife.

(13) It was a lethal Scrabble game. He put down all seven tiles on his first turn, and she, a brunette, throttled him. His word: B-L-O-N-D-E-S.

The View from Mt. Parnassus

Some of us prefer
not to travel
in flocks,

to live
inside our heads.
The other side of loneliness—

luxurious silence.
Slowed down,
you discover

your dog loves
sun-drenched spaces,
the twittering of birds,

just like you.
The paradox of
your particular

blessings and curses
astounds you. Plants, animals
make good friends. The body

knows all this
before the mind.
We humans are

smaller than
a hornet's nest
in the scheme of things.

Animation Moms

In forlorn January, I sit with other
        mothers of The Unusual
in semi-darkness, an alternative film class for kids.

Drowsy, sick of motherhood's fringe status, I'm
        saved by animation—
the children's paper cutouts instantly turned
        to motion by the woman teacher/film director, our saint.

With twenty-first century technology, my daughter's
        crimped, arthritic dragon
flies above autumnal trees, flapping his wings,

        undulating his spiked tail.
Almost graceful. Like our finger-tapping boys & girls
        in dark glasses and knitted ear flaps,
taken off Ritalin or Prozac, allowed to be floppy, jittery.

On the teacher's film screen, their objects jiggle & scatter,
        their humanoids flitter, cartwheel, limp. Like our hope.

Scarecrow

Isn't it grand to feel
the chill, to drape yourself
in scarves and hats?
The huge potted plant—
I forget its name—
flaunted gauche
red-purple gonads
in summer, and now
sits spidery, withered,
eccentric, just one flower
to mock itself. Pumpkins
defiantly glow beside
shattered stalks next door.
From my porch, I see
an unfamiliar man
struggle up the hill,
his legs crooked, gimpy.
Don't play the violins,
it's my neighbor friend—
gaunt scarecrow, gray thatch—
lugging his youngest child's
soccer gear to the school bus.
I just noticed that he's old.

Wasps

Not only the threat of the sting.
Your bodies, bulbous, hovering,
obscene, I loathe. Your angry
buzz, like lawyers arguing,
makes me cringe, move far away.

Perhaps you're excited
with your creation,
dark nest stuck
in the eaves,
an insect Mesa Verde.

Who can say humans are
dissimilar, with our
constant traffic whizzing
round skyscrapers?
Looking again at your home,

alive with crawling bodies,
I think barrios of Ecuador.
Brothels of Calcutta.
Stock exchanges.
Parliament. Or perhaps

you are monks,
droning a spiritual
syllable, loving your world.
Everywhere beings
sing their self-importance.

Panhandler Girl

Doowopbeebop gimme a little change
I'm flocacious and not so strange
Doodlybeebop I could be you

A little change is better than none
Nickels dimes quarters change
Lost a few years hitching bicoastal

Bivalve, bicuspid, bi-logical
Freakish fuckish
Be fantabulous give the poor snake girl

Some change   rearrange
You're so familiar I could be you
Be my famillionaire, rich uncle

Filthy Luke the Cur
took down my pants
He ain't breathin' no more

so who cares? Whoa,
zillionaire, change is good
but not so fast.

Freak your mono-mind. Change!
Doowopbeebop be my changer
into a straight A student

suckerpunch miss fancypants
goofballistic chick that's me
Just empty your piggish curse

into my lap, give me some
Change purse
I'll shimmer glimmer for you

with no pole
I ain't Polish or polished
I'm demolished, help me rebuild,

Uncle. Help me be scraped —
barnacles off the body politic —
don't be a frickly puck!

Ain't you ever been down and out?
Down in the muck?
Please, a little change

for some soup, bread,
place to rest my chowder head.
I'm flocacious and not so strange

I was once just like you
Doowopbeebop now I shufflestrut,
lunch me!
Monkey girl twirls
an invisible god

Be shrewd, dude – change for me and I'll
change for you. Glimglam flimflam
Snap my fingers: I'm you

Innocence Is Over Rated

Never look down on old ladies
who have not filled their homes
with new husbands. Their Old Men
are nowhere; children decamped
for odd places. Never look
down on old ladies nonchalantly
serving brandy eggnogs
as cats leap from sofa to
counter among crowds of
hand-painted dolls, cherubic
in their blushing freshness.

What we don't know
about old ladies–
their train journeys,
their impetuous
youths on horseback,
their daring rebellions,
their close calls with
death or deranged lovers…
Age should not
make us invisible.
Though cackling or chit-chat
may seem banal
over fine china and doilies,

can't we discern
the intrepid structures
they have erected,
the undefined spaces
left intact, all persons
allowed their disconsolate
secrets? Never look down on
old ladies. Take courage
from their dismantling
of intolerance,
served with lemon, sugar cubes,
on elegant dishes.

Everything but a Paycheck

Mother was a sonnet by Edna St. Vincent Millay.
She was a backhanded compliment,
a party girl and a Cliffie.
She was a lover of babies;
Mother was a rebel.
She was not The Church.
She was brightly colored ball gowns
from the Forties in the cedar closet.
She was "Big Noise From Winnetka."
She was books everywhere —
a dictionary in the dining room.
She was weeping and throwing things.
She was whispers about how to behave —
a hat and gloves to go to town,
art on the walls.
Mother was croquet in the backyard.
She was a naughty girl sent to Convent School.
She was poetry and nursery rhymes and stories.
Mother was The Beatles, whom she brought home first.
She was the apple of her father's eye, first born.
She was a gorgeous gal in New York City
during World War II
who went to librarian school
in case her Pilot Husband was blown from the sky
crossing the Himalayas, like most of his buddies.
Mother was dressing correctly for different occasions.
She was a secret never divulged.
She was a teenager in saddle shoes swooning
for Frank Sinatra.
She was a wedding proposal after Pearl Harbor.
She was Rosie the Riveter in a munitions factory in Chicago.
She was a nasty gossip and a poison pen letter.
She was a New England Town Meeting Member.
She was poetry books by Sylvia Plath and Anne Sexton
strewn about the house.
Mother was a very young toddler who lost her mother to twins. She
was temper tantrums; she was panic attacks;
she was sharp insults.
She was "Carpe Diem" and "Don't Take Any Wooden Nickels."
She was a black hole that sucked away happiness.
She was a very young woman who went with her Officer
Husband to deliver Bad News to many wives during Word War II —

"We got them in a car first because they always broke down." —
She was laughter; she was Emily Post;
she was everything but a paycheck.
She was the party and the clean-up service.
She was gypsy blood and "So he was a real Wolf"
when you came in bug-eyed.
She was knowing where you'd been
though you hadn't told her.
She was screaming from upstairs
when Professor stumbled home
drunk and held on to the walls, singing.
Mother was a fancy lunch made for the
Ironing Lady.
She was an avalanche of shoes
when Sister was dating.
She was a real dinner on the table every night
and the art of conversation.
She was an orange ceiling appearing in my bedroom
in the Sixties.
Mother was surprise, plot twist, the punch line;
she did everything right, but it came out wrong.
She was a put-down artist.
Mother knew how to talk to anybody.
She was Ginger Rogers dancing with Fred Astaire.
She was a ledger of all purchases —
60 cents for Keds —
which Daddy reviewed every night in their apartment.
She was no money but high social status.
She was Sargent Pepper's Lonely Hearts Club Band.
She brought ashtrays and drinks to Daddy,
always in high heels.

Blackbird's Wing

The afternoon meanders, a backwater kind of day,
in the gigolo networks for aging women
in Sarasota, Florida. A great career opportunity
for slightly too-old surfers and beach bums. Large green
fig leaves curve on her balcony. Country music plays softly
on the radio. *When she dies, she says she'll catch*
some blackbird's wing and fly away to heaven, come some
sweet blue bonnet spring... Garlic chicken strokes his nostrils,
cotton sheets caress him well enough. His afternoon sways
the way rock-and-roll moved for him after hashish in his teens.
She's thinking Marlon Brando as a young man, eyes closed,
his smokey voice, a café in Palermo, pistachio ice cream.
What a dead-end kinda job, to hump old ladies in beachfront condos!
He worked the oil rigs in the Gulf of Mexico, hawked hot dogs at
Disney World. You knew then when the cash was comin'.
He remembers young juicy sluts panting, their behinds ground
into sandy towels beneath palm trees, sneering moons.
One or two had told him of the blue sky-ocean of his eyes,
the wonder of his long blonde hair, slender sculpted torso.
All the way from Bumfuck, Tennessee, he'd come for this shit!
The luscious taste of avarice drips down his esophagus.
Do these two look as cherubic as children on Christmas morning?
They begin to read each others' thoughts, mortified, amused,
shaken. Could I get him to come back? I want to walk the beach.
In the mirror he sees a tender brute. This is, after all, about cash.
Sex always means more than just sex. Her ancient silver
brush-and-comb set recumbent on a doily sighs with the aftermath
of pleasure. He will crease fresh ATM bills into his salty wallet
and casually caress them down into his soft back blue jean pocket.

Our Anniversary

Our relationship is being reviewed in The Times.
They will say it can't compete with the hot new shows.

They don't understand the heart-pounding, nail-biting
meltdown. Our brains have sailed away. How far

would *you* go to look & feel younger?
I was a catch, the trap, a slender and streamlined

neurological disorder. Hey, creativity comes
as a result of handicap. You were an

uncensored romance with the geek squad,
a nugget of wisdom & electronics.

We're taking hologram vacations this year.
Who says you can't fall in love with

the history of emotions?

Fragment of Alaska

In morning light, fog drifts
near endless green arms
of Sitka spruce, hemlock.
Above innumerable giant trees,
sweet as incense, eagles circle
near snow-capped peaks,
stretching as far as we can see.

Our boat skims
over the narrow channel
between cliffs.
Humpback whales breach
off starboard,
just visible in the mist.

Upstream, spawned-out
carcasses of salmon
stink up stream banks
like thousands of cast-off
strange, dark jewels.
Their raw flesh
enriches animal, soil, tree.

As the sun rises higher,
the views make
the mind break
apart, calving glaciers
in sharp light,
a Sung dynasty painting
without the restraint
or hermit's hut.

Here you connect
differently from
the Lower Forty-Eight.
No roads between towns.
The wilderness will eat
you if you get lost.
Our thoughts are
seals asleep on blue
sculptured icebergs.
Slapping puny arms
stuck in fat parkas, pulling on

fur hats and gloves, we laugh,
tiny as ants, insignificant
before a vast glacier next to us.
Off port, waterfalls froth down
thousands of feet.
Heavy binoculars reveal
brown bears devouring
pink salmon roe onshore.
A pair of trumpeter swans
takes off, spreading
white wings
eight-feet wide.

Higher Education

If I ever get over my fear of slippery slopes,
I'm going to start sky-surfing.

Not how the mist looks from the earth,
but how it will look when

I matriculate at The University of Clouds
in its Ph.D. of Levity Program.

I'll be required to quit obsessing
about dogs, elections, and

water flowing over my body,
and to let go of pies, volcanoes,

and the death wishes of empires.
Our school buses will be seed pods.

Instead of reading books or dealing
with bodies, I'll be flight itself.

A few will crane their necks to watch
from the university stadium before I'm gone.

Without A Camera (Ghazal)

My friends in high school loved to take photographs.
I couldn't understand what was at stake. *Photographs?*

Writers like *words* better; subtleties more than surface.
If they didn't, wouldn't they just make photographs?

I often preferred black-and-white to color. Ansel Adams,
Diane Arbus capture their unique heartache in photographs.

Why do images assault or invade our minds?
Here's something crass, opaque: photographs.

"No ideas but in things," proclaimed William Carlos Williams.
I say to hell with snapshots — mentally forsake "photographs."

Wittgenstein knew: "The mystical is not *how* the world is,
but *that* it is." For you, let's have an Irish wake, photographs.

I am Karen, "pure" one, youngest of my posing, smiling clan.
I love and hate that shallow family keepsake — photographs.

Yet Another Surprise

A deep voice intones,
"You're on your
own now."
You have no idea
how the steering
apparatus works.
There's no manual.
No one offers help or
even water
for miles and miles.
The applause you remember
from long ago — muted
and oddly sporadic.
Out here, you don't
meet too many others,
and when you do
they sometimes
stare. Their parched lips
don't smile.
So this is *success*.
You'd thought
it would *be* something,
like paradise.

Buddha Out My Kitchen Window

When the acquaintance who may be one of those
who believes that the Bible is the *literal word of God*
looks out my kitchen window and sees the statue,
the graceful man sitting cross-legged beneath
the Japanese maple on my backyard ledge,
and asks me, "Are you Buddhist?"
I say no, I'm not. How could I be so arrogant
as to say I'm Buddhist? As soon as you've said it,
it seems to me, you've ceased to be one.
The same goes for Christian. Secretly, I think
I'm a bit of both. I like the Christian idea of loving
others without regard to their social station
because it's still radical and not widely practiced.
I also like the Buddhist idea that desire's the root
of our suffering and that we must practice
doing nothing, but that might be because
deep down I'm extremely lazy.
I'm Hindu because I love many goddesses
and Muslim when I want all these naked
starlets covered, for the one god's sake. Also,
Islam has great poetry, the ecstatic Sufi tradition. I'm
Taoist because I value emptiness, Jewish
when I contemplate the wisdom of the scroll.
Earth-based traditions appeal to me since
I'd like the earth to survive.
I'm all these religions including
atheist since how could there be a God when
there is so much bad taste?
Can't we pray while we wash dishes and
look out the kitchen window?

Torso with Leaves

A wood nymph
in the process of turning
from woman to leafy tree,
she moves in her
stillness, slender leaves
adhering to her breasts,
abdomen, thighs —
kind bandages,
gentle and soothing.

Her mottled breasts are
healing slowly
to beautiful bark,
her smooth, strong belly
ready for swaying,
her thighs majestic
as an ancient tree trunk.
She knows she will
thrive, despite

harsh scars, hospital visits.
Strong as a tree, she will
rise, emerald and gold
in the sun. Her gossamer
leaves will rustle,
no longer cradling her body,
but finally a shimmer —
scarlet orange
flying in autumn breeze.

The Shape of River in His Hands
for Andy Goldsworthy
"We need to learn to see our physical form as a river." –Thich Nhat Hanh

At art college he saw
artists in cubicles.
He walked outside,
went to work
on the beach:
cones of stone,
driftwood caves,
rivers of stone,
of leaf, of clay.

He records
his ephemera
in the language of
photography.
The sculptures
themselves
change & disappear quickly
due to tides, sun, wind, rain.
Sometimes they
collapse during creation —
spiraling twigs connected
to a tree
fall to the ground —
he slumps in despair
for a moment.

He plays
like a river,
curve after curve,
to the salty ocean.
A hole in dark rocks
he fills with
bright yellow
dandelion flowers
he has picked
near gray waterfalls,
the yellow a shock,
an offering.

He says, "I don't think
the land needs me at all,
but I need it."
Sun brings his
icicle sculptures
wrapped around
branches
to life
and to death.
He says, "I'm so
amazed at times
that I'm actually alive,"
as his bruised,
scratched-up hands
keep moving.

That Kitchen Bravery Thing

My daughter is canoeing downstream
in the bathtub. When I ask her what
she's doing, dipping her paddle again
and again, she replies, "You know,
that kitchen bravery thing."

When I return, she exclaims,
"I'm stirring a pot of men!"
Which she is in fact doing –
vigorously churning chunky dolls
in a plastic pot. "You're wonderful,"
I hear myself say. Inane adult.

"I'm not wonderful," she yells,
"I'm spicy!"

To be so brazen,
stirring ingredients
to an unknown
conclusion, and then
to dance naked,
a towel sailing
behind me
down the hall!

Fin

Acknowledgments

Many thanks to the editors of the following journals and magazines where some of these poems, sometimes in earlier versions, appeared or will appear:

"The Live-In" in *Astarte,*

"Ars Poetica: A Charm of Hummingbirds," "Scarecrow," and "Yellow Orchid" in *The Avocet,*

"Amethyst" won a poetry prize in the national Dancing Poetry Contest, San Francisco,

"A Spine Moving," "The Prize," and "Why I Can't Go Back to My High-Tech Cubicle" in *Caveat Lector,*

"Impossibly Huge Female" in *Diner,*

"Higher Education," "My Favorite Incarnations," "Trumpet Flower Vine in August" in *Emerald Coast Review,*

"Kept" in *Fireweed,*

"Never" in *Grolier Poetry Prize Annual,*

"When We Were Flying Fish" in *Hipfish,*

"The Tyranny of Women" and "Without A Camera" in *Iconoclast,*

"Tree Music," "To Visit with the Grape Hyacinth," and "Hiking in the Sonoran Desert" in *In the Mist,*

"Animation Moms" in *Literary Mama,*

"Lifting Off" in *Mefisto* (English and Italian),

"Stone Heart" in *Oregon Review,*

"Dominatrix Month-by-Month Planner" in *Panoply,*

"Mona Lisa Discusses Money" and "Poem Written in a Copy of *The Aeneid*" in *Poem,*

"Wasps" in *Pool,*

"Iphigenia, Coming On Fast" in *The Spoon River Poetry Review,*

"Thirteen Noir Tweets" first published on Twitter where I published a "noir tweet" every day for a year and a half,

"My First Job" in *Untitled Country*,

"Menopause" in *Verseweavers*,

"The Swan Boats," "Couple with Ginger Lilies," and "Buddha Out My Kitchen Window" in *The Worcester Review*.

About the Author

Karen Braucher Tobin is the author of three full-length poetry collections, *Grit & Whimsy*, *Aqua Curves*, and *Sending Messages Over Inconceivable Distances*, as well as two chapbooks, *Heaven's Net* and *Mermaid Café*. Her poems have been published in many places including *Caveat Lector*, *Literary Mama*, *Nervy Girl*, *Nimrod*, *The Oregonian*, *Oregon Review*, *Poem, Pool*, *Rattle*, *The Spoon River Poetry Review*, and *The Worcester Review*, as well as anthologies. They've won regional and national prizes, including two Oregon Literary Arts fellowships, the Grolier Poetry Prize, the Worcester Poetry Prize, The Bacchae Press national chapbook prize, and the national Stevens Poetry Prize for *Aqua Curves* (Peter Meinke, judge). One of her poems appeared on Portland, Oregon's trains and buses through the national Poetry in Motion program. Her poetry collection about adopting her daughter from China, *Sending Messages Over Inconceivable Distances*, made the "Oregon 150 Poetry Books List," compiled by *Poetry Northwest*. She is also the author of a satiric mystery, *Poetic License to Kill* (Salvo Press), set in Portland, Oregon, and featuring mother-daughter amateur sleuths. She has taught many writing workshops for adults and children, and also tutors high school students. For ten years she was editor and publisher of the Portlandia chapbook series, a national contest for poets. She lives with her family in Oregon.